# Animal Icons ·
# BALD EAGLES

Sheila Griffin Llanas

**ABDO Publishing Company**

## visit us at
## www.abdopublishing.com

Printed in the United States of America, North Mankato, Minnesota.
112012
012013

 PRINTED ON RECYCLED PAPER

Cover Photo: Michael Melford/National Geographic Stock
Interior Photos: Alamy pp. 1, 12–13, 15, 17, 24–25, 26–27; Corbis pp. 14–15, 16–17, 18–19,
        20–21, 27, 28–29; iStockphoto pp. 6–7, 8, 9; Roy Toft/National Geographic Stock pp. 22–23;
        Thinkstock pp. 4–5; Tom Murphy/National Geographic Stock pp. 10–11

Editors: Rochelle Baltzer, Tamara L. Britton, Megan M. Gunderson
Art Direction: Neil Klinepier

### Cataloging-in-Publication Data

Llanas, Sheila Griffin, 1958-
 Bald eagles / Sheila Griffin Llanas.
   p. cm. -- (Animal icons)
Includes bibliographical references and index.
ISBN 978-1-61783-568-1
1. Bald eagle--Juvenile literature.   I. Title.
598.9/45--dc22

                                                    2012946541

# CONTENTS

# BALD EAGLES

In the Tlingit language, *Chilkat* means "storage container for salmon." Five species of salmon **spawn** in Alaska's Chilkat River. After spawning, the salmon die. More than 3,000 bald eagles feast on the carcasses.

On a map, the river looks small. But no other place in the world attracts this many bald eagles. Today, the Alaska Chilkat Bald Eagle Preserve protects this **habitat**.

The eagle population has not always prospered. At one time, their numbers were so few that they were declared an **endangered** species. Conservation efforts and habitat preservation led to an amazing comeback.

Today, the bald eagle is a powerful symbol. It is sacred to many native peoples. It is the national symbol and national bird of the United States. The bald eagle is an animal icon.

An icon is a cultural symbol. Animal icons stand for the people and land of nations, states, and cities. Animal icons are shown on flags and signs. They appear in songs, legends, and stories. They represent history. They teach people about nature and about themselves.

# BALD EAGLE
# HISTORY

There are about 60 eagle species in the world. Only two live in North America. They are the golden eagle and the bald eagle. The bald eagle is the only species native to the continent.

Many Native American tribes considered the bald eagle to be a magical bird. Bald eagles represented truth and majesty, courage and wisdom. As medicine birds, they also had healing powers. The bald eagle was a **clan** totem in many tribes. Tribes with eagle clans include the Tsimshian, Chippewa, and Osage.

Bald eagle feathers were also spiritual icons. Tribe members gave the feathers as badges of honor. The feathers were placed in war bonnets and headdresses.

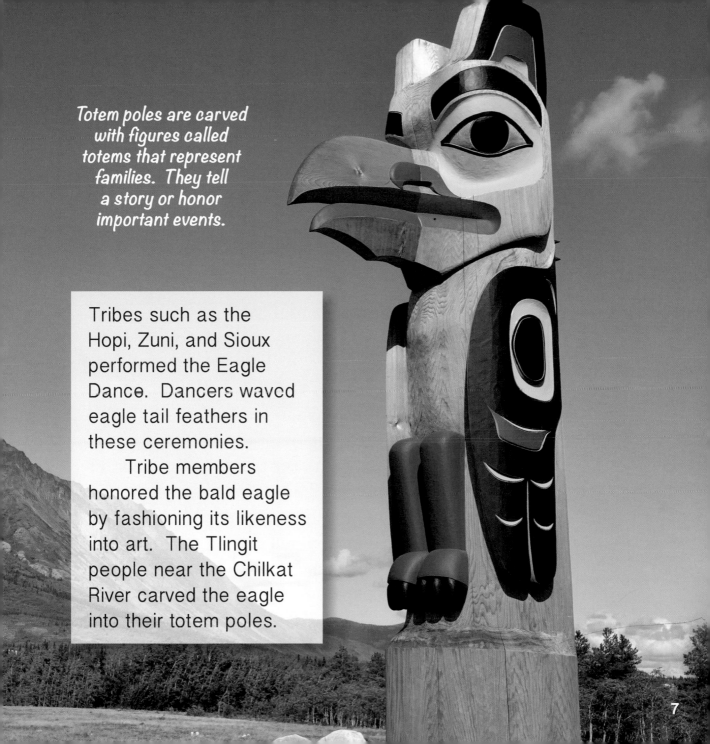

Totem poles are carved with figures called totems that represent families. They tell a story or honor important events.

Tribes such as the Hopi, Zuni, and Sioux performed the Eagle Dance. Dancers waved eagle tail feathers in these ceremonies.

Tribe members honored the bald eagle by fashioning its likeness into art. The Tlingit people near the Chilkat River carved the eagle into their totem poles.

When the United States was a young country, Congress wanted a seal for the new nation. In 1776, John Adams, Thomas Jefferson, and Benjamin Franklin were asked to select a design.

The men considered biblical figures, Greek gods, and **Saxon** chiefs. But they could not agree on one.

In 1782, a new committee was formed. Charles Thompson and William Barton produced a design with an eagle holding the U.S. flag. That year, the bald eagle became the nation's official emblem on June 20.

At the time, as many as 75,000 bald eagles soared in what is now the lower 48 states. But as the nation expanded westward, the bald eagle suffered. Settlers cut down the tall trees that provided nesting sites. Towns were established near rivers and lakes where eagles hunted for food. Eagle hunting sites were filled with trains, steamships, boats, and dams.

*There are two subspecies of bald eagle. They are the Northern Bald Eagle and the Southern Bald Eagle.*

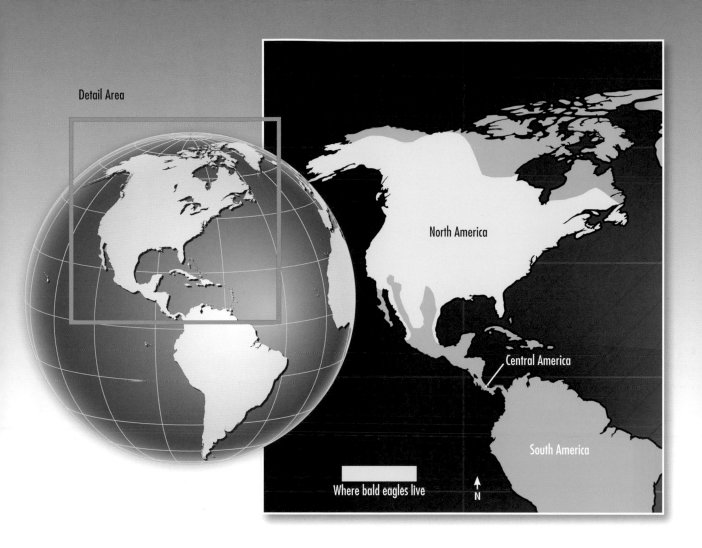

Detail Area

North America

Central America

South America

Where bald eagles live

N

By 1900, bald eagles were scarce. To help increase their population, the U.S. government passed the Bald and Golden Eagle Protection Act in 1940. This law made it illegal to kill bald eagles.

# MORE LORE

But even with the new law, the bald eagle population continued to decline. Why? Scientists worked to solve the mystery.

In the 1940s, a **pesticide** called DDT was developed. Farmers sprayed DDT on crops. Gardeners used it on their vegetables. Governments used it for insect control.

The chemical did some good. It eliminated mosquitoes, insects that can carry **malaria**. However, insect pests became resistant to DDT. In addition, DDT hurt the **environment**. It traveled long distances in the atmosphere. Runoff collected DDT in waterways.

Fish, mice, and songbirds ate the poisoned insects and plants. Bald eagles ate the toxic fish, mice, and songbirds. They drank the toxic water. This caused high levels of DDT to build up in their bodies. Worse, DDT does not dissolve in water. So, bald eagles could not flush it out of their systems.

The United States and the United Nations are working together to end the use of DDT worldwide.

Their population has recovered. Still, 30 percent of bald eagles do not survive their first year of life due to sickness, lack of food, and human interference.

The DDT in the eagles' bodies affected the eggs they laid. The eggs had thin shells. The shells broke before the eaglets were ready to hatch. By the 1960s, only 900 eagles remained in the lower 48 United States.

In 1972, the U.S. government took action. DDT was banned. The Bald and Golden Eagle Protection Act was strengthened. A person who harmed a bald eagle could get fined up to $100,000. Jail time could amount to a year or more. A second offense would be a **felony**. And in 1978, the bald eagle was declared an **endangered** species.

Those conservation and protection efforts paid off. In just ten years, the bald eagle recovered. The population in the wild grew healthy again. In 2007, bald eagles were removed from the Endangered Species List. Today, there are 9,789 nesting pairs in the lower 48 United States.

# BEAK TO TALONS

In many animal species, males are larger than females. But for bald eagles, the opposite is true. Males are 36 inches (92 cm) long. They have a wingspan of about 6.5 feet (2 m). Female bald eagles are about 43 inches (109 cm) long. Their wingspan is 8 feet (2.4 m).

The bodies of bald eagles are covered with dark brown feathers. The feathers on their heads and tails are white. The layers of dark feathers hold in warmth in cold weather. They let cool air in during hot weather.

Bald eagles have yellow eyes, beaks, and feet. The curved beak is more than 2 inches (5 cm) long. It is sharp and easily tears up prey.

The bald eagle's feet have three front toes and one back toe. Eagles use their toes to grab and grip, like you use your hands. On the tip of each toe is a black talon. Bald Eagles use these sharp claws to seize and kill prey.

## BALD EAGLE TAXONOMY

Kingdom: Animalia
Phylum: Chordata
Class: Aves
Order: Falconformes
Family: Accipitridae
Genus: Haliaeetus
Species: Haliaeetus
         Leucocephalus

*Rain runs off of a bald eagle's feathers but snow sticks to them. Bald eagles get wetter in snow than in rain.*

# WHAT'S FOR DINNER?

Bald eagles are carnivores. They hunt small birds, mammals, snakes, turtles, and crabs. They also eat **carrion**. But, the bald eagle's preferred meal is fish.

When hunting for fish, bald eagles glide above the water. They use their talons to grab and kill live fish.

Bald eagles will steal food even when it is plentiful. They rob fish from better hunters, such as ospreys. They even steal from fellow bald eagles!

Eagles have a pouch in their throats called a crop. They can carry food in the crop to a safer eating place. The crop is also used to store food.

In the crop, bones and hair are sorted from the prey. Food goes on into the eagle's stomach. Whatever cannot be **digested** stays in the crop. The bald eagle **vomits** this waste.

Bald eagles can eat fish from both fresh and salt water.

A bald eagle can lift about four pounds (1.8 kg). It can eat one pound (0.5 kg) of fish in four minutes.

# BALD EAGLE
# BEHAVIOR

Bald eagles can live in forests, deserts, mountains, or prairies. But they need water to survive. So, bald eagles must live near water.

The distance from water depends on a bald eagle's **habitat**. For example, in Alaska, 99 percent of bald eagles live just 45 yards (40 m) from a shoreline. Florida birds nest about two miles (3 km) from water. In Minnesota and Oregon, bald eagles can be as many as four miles (7 km) from a body of water.

Bald eagles defend their body of water. It is their territory. Other eagles that dare to fly too close get a midair chase!

When fighting, eagles use their sharp talons as weapons. This protects their faces, eyes, and beaks from injury. But it can be fatal to one or both eagles.

Bald eagles can fly up to 60 miles per hour (97 km/h)! They can dive even faster. Diving eagles can reach speeds of up to 100 miles per hour (161 km/h).

Bald eagles are famous for soaring on thermal columns. These rising currents of warm air can lift them up to 10,000 feet (3,000 m) in the air.

# BIRTH TO DEATH

Bald eagles build their nests in tall trees or on rock **pinnacles**. The nests are about five feet (1.5 m) wide. They are flat, not bowl-shaped like some other birds' nests. Bald eagles may use the same nest for many years. Each year, they add more branches to the nest.

To build a nest, bald eagle pairs layer sticks into a platform. They use live branches up to six feet (2 m) long. Dead branches are too dry to use because they break easily. A layer of soft plants lines the inside of the nest. Grasses, pine boughs, leaves, and cattails make a soft mattress.

*Bald eagle pairs begin building a nest one to three months before the female lays her eggs.*

Mating season depends on the weather. In the Great Plains and mountain states, eagles nest from January to March. In Alaska, they nest from March to May.

One week after mating, the female begins to lay eggs. She lays one egg every two days. She will lay two or three eggs. The white, oval-shaped eggs are the size of baseballs.

Both parents **incubate** the eggs to protect them and keep them warm. This is an important job. If the eggs get cold, the eaglets could die. If a predator reaches the nest, it will eat the eggs. It hardly stands a chance though! Bald eagles are quick to fight off any predators.

Eaglets are covered with light gray down. Fledglings have brown feathers. A mature bald eagle will have a white head and tail when it is about five years old.

Bald eagles have two seasons, nesting and roosting. During nesting they raise chicks together. During roosting they live alone.

After a month of **incubation**, the eaglets hatch. Each eaglet uses its egg tooth to break its eggshell. It spends from twelve to forty-eight hours chipping away.

The new eaglets are wet and helpless. Both parents incubate and protect them. They curl their toes into balls so their talons will not cut the eaglets. The parents spread their wings to shield them from sun and rain.

After a few days, the eaglets become nestlings. Both parents feed them. But the male does the most hunting. He carries food to the nest. There, he and the female tear the food up and feed it to the nestlings.

At three months old, nestlings become fledglings. At this time, they are ready for short trial flights. By the end of the summer, the fledglings have left the nest. They must fly and hunt to survive on their own.

The nesting cycle takes about 20 weeks. When nesting season ends, the parents split up. Bald eagle pairs do not **migrate** together. They go their separate ways.

If eaglets survive to adulthood, they can have long lives. Bald eagles can live to be 30 years old.

# THE ICONIC BALD EAGLE

Today, the bald eagle is the main image on the Great Seal of the United States. It appears on the front of the seal.

The group of stars at the top symbolizes the country taking its place among the world's nations. A banner in the eagle's beak reads *E Pluribus Unum*. This Latin phrase means "Out of many, one."

Clutched in the eagle's right talons is an olive branch for peace. The bundle of arrows in its left talons stands for war. On the eagle's shield, 13 stripes represent the original colonies. The blue bar above it represents Congress.

In 1969, the National Aeronautics and Space Administration (NASA) launched the Apollo 11 mission. Part of the spacecraft was named the Eagle. When the Eagle reached the moon's surface, astronaut Neil Armstrong declared, "The Eagle has landed."

President Ronald Reagan named 1982 the Bicentennial Year of the American Bald Eagle.

A bald eagle's head isn't bald, it is covered with white feathers. So why does it have that name? It comes from balde, an Old English word for white.

The bald eagle is a symbol of pride for the U.S. military. Many military service rings carry the image of a bald eagle. Statues of eagles grace veterans memorials and grave sites.

On September 11, 2001, **terrorists** attacked New York, Pennsylvania, and Washington, DC. Eagle Rock Reservation park in West Orange, New Jersey, faces the New York City skyline. From there, citizens watched the events unfold in New York City.

In 2002, the Remembrance and Rebirth memorial was opened at Eagle Rock. A statue of a bronze bald eagle spreads its wings. Beneath it is a book that lists the names of those from Essex County who died on that fateful day.

On July 14, 2010, the Confederated Salish and Kootenai Tribes opened the Eagle Circle veterans monument in Pablo, Montana. An eagle is carved on a ten-foot (3-m) wall of black granite. Its wings enclose other sacred icons such as coyotes and buffaloes. The memorial honors more than 1,200 Flathead Reservation veterans.

# INTO THE FUTURE

Eagle feathers are a symbol of honor in many Native American **cultures**. Tribes use them in marriages, funerals, and other ceremonies. Feathers are awarded to students who reach educational goals. They are given for other successes, too.

However, the Bald and Golden Eagle Protection Act makes it illegal to possess any part of an eagle without permission. So for some time, Native Americans had no feathers to use in ceremonies.

In 1994, the U.S. government granted tribes the right to possess feathers for religious purposes. On October 12, 2012, a new policy clarified obtaining, possessing, and transporting bald eagle feathers and parts. Today, tribe members may request feathers from the National Eagle Repository.

For now, protection efforts have saved the bald eagle from extinction. To continue conservation efforts, it is important to learn more about this amazing bird.

In 2005, the first bald eagle nest was recovered from the wild. It was put on display at Jackson Bottom Wetlands Education Center in Hillsboro, Oregon. There, visitors can get a close look at a bald eagle's home.

In 2009, the Raptor Resource Center placed a camera in a bald eagle nest in Decorah, Iowa. In 2011, they streamed the images on the Internet. Millions of people from 184 countries tuned in. They saw the female eagle lay eggs. They watched as the eggs hatched and the downy eaglets grew into fledglings.

The bald eagle represents the strength and courage of the nation. To native peoples, the magical eagle is a symbol of truth, courage, and wisdom. The bald eagle is an animal icon.

# GLOSSARY

**carrion** - dead, rotting flesh.

**clan** - an extended family sharing a common ancestor.

**culture** - the customs, arts, and tools of a nation or a people at a certain time.

**digest** - to break down food into simpler substances the body can absorb. Digestion is the process of digesting.

**endangered** - in danger of becoming extinct.

**environment** - all the surroundings that affect the growth and well-being of a living thing.

**felony** - a serious crime.

**habitat** - a place where a living thing is naturally found.

**incubate** - to keep eggs warm so they will hatch.

**malaria** - a disease spread by certain mosquitoes. It causes chills and fever.

**migrate** - to move from one place to another, often to find food.

**pesticide** (PEHS-tuh-side) - a substance used to destroy pests.

**pinnacle** - the peak of a mountain or a rock formation.

**Saxon** - a Germanic people who entered and conquered England in the 400s.

**spawn** - to produce or deposit eggs.

**terrorist** - a person who uses violence to threaten people or governments.

**vomit** - the act of rejecting the contents of the stomach out through the mouth.

# WEB SITES

To learn more about bald eagles, visit ABDO Publishing Company online. Web sites about bald eagles are featured on our Book Links page. These links are routinely monitored and updated to provide the most current information available.

**www.abdopublishing.com**

# INDEX